A Note from Tricia

You might change a life by picking up this handbook. That's not an exaggeration. You're reading these pages because you want to help. Maybe you already have a teen mom in mind. Maybe you have yet to learn who God is going to bring your way. But you care, and believe it or not, that's what teen moms need the most. Yes, they need diapers, babysitters, and advice, but even more than those things they need to know someone loves them. Someone cares.

I created this handbook as a companion to *Teen Mom: You're Stronger Than You Think*, to give parents, family, mentors, and church leaders a resource to help the teen mom in their lives. In this handbook I share more about the love of some important women during my pregnancy--women who pointed me to Christ. But first I want to offer some encouragement (and a little reality check).

- ~ Teen moms will need more help than you can provide.
- ~ Some day you won't have all the answers.
- ~ Other days you'll wonder why you thought reaching out to young moms was a good idea.
- ~ You'll often feel as if you're in over your head.

But there's even a bigger reality than that! In your weak moments don't let worries and fears crowd in. Instead, know that where you are weak God is strong. Believe all your efforts, as hesitant as they may be, can forever change a young woman's life.

I know this because my life was changed by someone just like you.

- ~ Your love can point a young woman to the love of God.
- ~ Your example can help her learn to be a good mom.
- ~ Your kind words can help her get through tough days.
- ~ Your support can teach her how to support others.
- ~ And maybe someday your love for Jesus will be hers too.

I hope this handbook will help you in your service to teen moms. Remember when you reach out to a teen mom, you're getting a two-for-one. You're not only forever impacting a mom . . . you're positively impacting her child too!

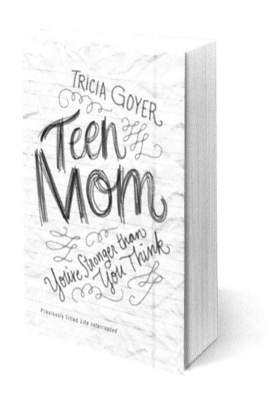

Teen Mom:
You're Stronger Than You Think

Do you want to help young moms, but you don't know how? In *Teen Mom: You're Stronger Than You Think,* Tricia Goyer speaks to the heart of young mothers. A mom at age 17, Tricia remembers what it felt like to carry the weight of the world on her shoulders. She's also been the coordinator of a teen mom support group for over twelve years, and she's cheered on many young moms—from all walks of life—through their journey.

In *Teen Mom,* Tricia pours out her heart and shares advice for the hard things young moms face. She hopes this book will provide encouragement, truth, and helpful resources to young moms and their families, church leaders, mentors, and friends.

Tricia suggests having a copy of *Teen Mom* for yourself and for the teen mom in your life, so you can read through the book together.

Check out the companion workbook, too! It's available for free digitally.

Purchasing in Bulk

If you're planning on buying copies of Teen Mom, you're eligible for free shipping and the following discounts:

1-20 copies: 30%
21-99 copies: 40%
100+ copies: 50%

Order at ChurchSource.com, or call 800-727-3480. Use promo code TEENMOM. Offer expires December 31, 2015.

Chapter 1

Background to Teen Mom: An Unexpected Life

Growing up I liked to imagine what my future would be like. I imagined living in the small, California town I grew up in. I pictured getting married, having a few children, and teaching elementary school. None of that came true. Not even close. Instead, I became a teen mom, having my son at age seventeen. Becoming a mom at a young age was hard, but it also drew me to God. When I was six months pregnant I turned my life over to Him, and I started praying for my future husband.

God answered that prayer quickly. John was my pastor's son, and he came to visit me after Cory's birth. I knew a good thing when I saw it, and I didn't let John get away. We married when Cory was nine months old (in 1990), and we soon had two more children. We got involved in church, and I started pursuing writing, focusing on Christian books and magazine articles—but my efforts didn't get me far. And it wasn't for lack of effort. I worked and worked, and even though I got lots of articles published, book contracts were nonexistent.

I was frustrated because I was trying to move forward with my life. I wanted to prove I hadn't messed up my life by becoming a teen mom. What I realize now is that God was asking me to look back for a reason. First He wanted to bring me healing after an abortion I had at age fifteen (something I regret but found healing for).

Then I felt God's urging to help young women who were facing teen pregnancy. I put my writing to the side to help start a crisis pregnancy center and start a teen mom support group. Lives were changed, and God was using my mess to share a message. It wasn't what I planned, but God brought in people to join the cause.

When sharing "who" I am, I always have to share the challenging parts of my story first, mostly because who I am is ONLY because of who God is. When I took control of my life, I made a complete mess of it. When I gave my life over to God, He led me down paths I never envisioned—taking me on amazing journeys!

God just didn't patch things up so my dreams could come true. Instead, God had bigger and grander plans. He is the creator of everything, including great dreams for His children.

Today, all my publication dreams have come true. I've had more than 500 articles published in magazines and more than 50 books with publishers like Random House, HarperCollins, Focus on the Family, and Tyndale. I've won awards and made the best-sellers list. I love writing, but that's only a small part of who I am.

You see, I did not travel on this writing journey alone. When God put writing on my heart, I was a mom of three young kids. I wrote before they woke up, during nap times and quiet times, and after they went to bed.

As a homeschooling mom, my kids were part of all of it. They've been on research trips with me, and they've met amazing people. They volunteered at the pregnancy center and sat across the table with World War II veterans, listening to their stories. And their dad has always been there too, helping me balance everything and cheering me on.

I'm a full-time wife and full-time, homeschooling mom of six children, ranging in ages 25–4. I'm also a full-time writer. And I mentor teen moms on the side. Three of our children were adopted, and I'm greatly enjoying having little ones in the house again after raising the three older kids. (We're also in the process of adopting four more kids!) You know I love the mothering part of my life if I wanted to do it again!

People ask me how I do it all, and I tell them I can't do any of it without God. But there's more to it than that. I've seen what God has done with my life, and I'm greatly enjoying this ride. My husband and I have always said we don't want to miss out on one thing that God has for us.

I'd rather go to bed weary every night, seeing how God has used me in numerous ways, than trying to build a comfortable life.

My work isn't easy— being a wife, a mother, a writer, or a mentor—but all the places I'm weak give God room to shine.

Nothing about my life is expected, and isn't that amazing?! God has given me an unexpected life, filled with unexpected blessings.

It's not a perfect life. It's not an easy life. Not even close. But my prayer is I'll continue to be able to share how God turned my mess into my message, to anyone willing to listen, especially teen moms. After all, He gets all the glory from that!

Each of us has an unexpected life, don't we? We don't often end up on the exact path we imagined as a child. Instead we face low valleys and high spots. We've been hurt, and we've found joy. Life is harder than we thought—yet better too.

When we set our vision on helping teen moms, it's important to share ALL our story. So many times leaders and mentors try to approach teen moms putting on their best show. This isn't needed. In fact, this could even hinder the relationship you're trying to build with young moms. They feel far from perfect, and they want to see how you handle your flaws, your weaknesses, and your regrets.

Be open and share your story—and not just the good parts. As you do, young moms will learn to trust you. They'll open up their hearts because they know you're someone who understands.

Your Turn:

1. What's your story? Embrace it, and remember it's made you who you are.
2. Be open and vulnerable. Remember, others may be struggling with the same thing you've experienced.
3. Spend time reflecting on the gifts you've been given and thanking God for them!

Chapter 2

Someone Needs to Hear: Will You Tell Her?

It's easy to get excited about working with teenage mothers. It makes sense in our minds.

- When we help a young woman, we're not only helping her but also her child.
- Reaching out to teen moms is a modern-day way of caring for "orphans and widows."
- Loving teen moms is truly following God's commands of helping "the least of these."

The thing is that teen moms often need more help than we expect. They also might not make positive changes as quickly as we hope they'd would. Then—even if they do make positive changes—they often revert to their old ways. (Sigh.)

Throughout the years I've learned this ministry is one of planting seeds of truth. Sometimes we see those seeds take root. Many times we don't. Sometimes it takes years and years before we see the fruit of our efforts. (It's cool when it happens like that!)

And then . . . when you least expect it . . . a young woman will make a decision to follow God. And it will show you that every moment you spend is worth it! I wanted to share one of those stories with you to encourage you on days when you question why you're doing all you're doing.

Liz's Story

Last night I sat in a small support group of teenage mothers, and one brave young woman, Liz, walked to the front of the room.

"Guys, I usually sit there among you, but I asked Miss Tricia if I could share. You see, I've started this journey with Jesus, and I have to share all the amazing things God has done for me."

Less than four months ago Liz showed up at our group with a dump truck of sin weighing down her heart. She was so ashamed of her recent mistakes that she'd missed many meetings. Yet a glimmer of hope stirred inside. **Go to them, and ask for prayer; maybe they'll still love you.**

The first night back, Liz took me aside, and we found a quiet room. She poured out her heart, and I cried along with her. Then she prayed and accepted Christ in her heart.

As I led her in that prayer I could feel the weights lifting: pain, shame, disgrace . . . they were boulders being hurled from her back. We stood and embraced, and the light on her face reflected the transformation in her heart. She prayed and asked God to take over, and He did. Man, how He did!

"You'll never believe all God's done for me. He's provided people to care for me, to mentor me, and He's taken care of all my needs and the needs of my two kids." Liz walked away from unhealthy relationships and discovered a community of Christians. She's a different mom, a different student, a different friend.

"If you want to join me on my journey, call me whenever you want or text me. Come over, and we'll read the Bible together. There's so much He has for you."

As I sat and listened with tears in my eyes, I realized every moment I've spent volunteering in these teen mom support groups was worth it. It was worth it because Liz is worth it . . . and so is every other young mom who needs to hear the truth of Jesus' love.

I've been honored to watch these stories of transformation unfold, but that's only happened because deep down I knew there was someone out there who needed to hear. There is someone in your community who needs to hear, too. Someone who feels alone. Someone who feels unworthy. Someone who feels ashamed.

Somebody needs to hear . . . they are worth your time.
Somebody needs to hear . . . God's grace is for them.
Somebody needs to hear . . . their darkest sins are not too dark for God's light.
Somebody needs to hear . . . there is hope.
Somebody needs to hear . . . peace can come.
Somebody needs to hear . . . about a second chance through Jesus.

But before they can hear all those things, they must hear something from you first.

Things like:
Do you want to meet for coffee?
How can I help you?
What do you need most right now?
What's your story?
Do you want to hear how I've messed up?
Do you want to hear what God did?

People need to hear about Jesus, and it's hard to take the time, energy, and even money to make that a priority.

As I leave home and drive to our Thursday night meetings, I'm lucky if I've slapped together peanut butter and jelly for my husband and kids. I've stepped out of movies to take desperate phone calls. I've bought food, diapers, and door prizes to draw in the young women who need help, and I've asked myself, "Will they ever understand?" when it seems like they won't.

But I continue because I know someone needs to hear . . . and if I don't tell them, who will?

I also remember being the one who needed to hear about Jesus' love and forgiveness when I was a soon-to-be mom at age seventeen. Somebody talked to me, and it cost them too. *Was it worth the cost? Was I worth the cost?* I feel it was. I feel I am.

"Take up your cross and follow me," Jesus said, and in 2015 that looks a little different than what it did in Jesus' day. It might mean asking a friend to drive your child to t-ball practice, or walking away from that pile of dishes, or spending hard-earned cash to hire a babysitter for two hours so you can take someone out just to talk.

Sacrifice is sacrifice, big or small. But transformation is TRANSFORMATION in the lives Jesus touches through you. Without us stepping out and doing our part, who's going to tell them? Who's going to tell her?

And without being told how, will they know Who to follow?

And if they don't know Who do follow, where will they wander? Into sin, pain, darkness, shame, and regret. It's easier to shake our head at their choices than to reach out and be a friend. Because it costs us something, doesn't it?

Will you do it? Will you speak? Will you give? Will you love?

 Your Turn:

1. Who has God placed in your life you need to reach out to? Spend time praying for that person and guidance.
2. What words do you need to say to that person? Would you like to get coffee? How can I help You?
3. Be bold and say them!

Some days it might be hard to serve in this ministry, but stories like Liz's remind us it's all worth it.

Chapter 3

How to Start a MOPS Group

If you've followed me for any time on Facebook (@AuthorTriciaGoyer) or Twitter (@TriciaGoyer), you've heard me talk about Teen MOPS. Teen MOPS is a support group for teenage mothers. It's part of MOPS International (www.mops.org).

What Is Teen MOPS?

Teen MOPS is a support group for our youngest moms. I started a Teen MOPS group in Kalispell, Montana, in 2000. After moving to Little Rock in 2010, I started a group here too.

- If you'd like to find out how to start a Teen MOPS group, visit mops.org/start-a-group.
- Teen MOPS groups are run similarly to MOPS groups. There is food, a game, a short devotion, a speaker or activity, and discussion groups. Groups can meet weekly or bi-weekly. Our group here in Little Rock runs weekly. We do this because it was hard for young moms to remember which week as "on" and which was "off." Our meetings start at 6:00 with shopping. Dinner starts at 6:20. The meeting itself starts at 6:40 and ends at 7:30. We have leaders' meetings every month, usually on Sunday afternoons.
- Teen MOPS is run by volunteer leaders. They can be women with young kids or older kids. We've had volunteers who don't have kids yet. Volunteers can be retired women or women in college. We even have high schoolers who help with child care and other needs we have. I got involved in Teen MOPS because I was a teen mom . . . but you don't have to be a former teen mom to volunteer. Women who volunteer do so for various reasons. You just need to come to the meetings with an open heart and outstretched arms.
- At our meetings we provide a dinner for our moms. We provide childcare, and we have a "baby store." Young moms earn MOPS dollars for coming, bringing a friend, going to doctor visits, etc. Every meeting they can take home diapers or clothes.
- After I started a Teen MOPS group I realized there was a need for a book just for them. That's why I wrote *Teen Mom: You're Stronger Than You Think*. I also have other resources available at: www.TriciaGoyer.com/teen-mom. MOPS International also has wonderful resources!

How to Start

- Talk to your church or a local crisis pregnancy about starting the group. Pick a meeting space.
- Set a schedule and write out your mission and goals.
- Talk to ladies about volunteering. To get the word out I posted announcements in bulletins, talked on local Christian radio, and spoke at local groups. Local MOPS groups also give awesome help and support! I've gotten some great volunteers from these groups.

- Get funding. Local churches can help. Small groups or other community groups can help too. (I run our group on less than $400 a month. We get people to donate food, donate childcare, donate door prizes, etc. I also get folks to buy and donate copies of *Teen Mom* to our group.)
- Make a brochure or flyer and send it out. I send it to hospitals, doctors, social service agencies, schools, churches, etc.
- Plan the meetings. Teen MOPS groups usually run on a school-year schedule from September–May.
- Advertise. Put up posters. Send press releases about your group to newspapers and community calendars.
- Pray. (Actually pray with each step!)
- Be patient. When Teen MOPS starts it may take a while to grow. We often start with two-to-five girls each meeting.
- Love on the girls. You can plan and plan, but your love is what will keep them coming back!

Your Turn:

1. Are you interested in starting a teen MOPS group?
2. Who can help you lead a group?
3. Who do you need to invite to the group?
4. Pray about it and pursue the needed steps to make it happen!

Remember: You don't need to have everything figured out to start. You just have to take the first step!

Chapter 4

5 Practical Steps to Running a Teen MOPS Group

I've been running a Teen MOPS group for 13 years, and even though the teen moms now have smart phones, take selfies, and connect with each other (and us leaders) on Facebook and Instagram, nothing much has changed about our group format for the last decade. Why? From the beginning, I tried to figure out what the basic needs of teen moms were and how we could meet them. And it's worked! We've had successful groups, and we've seen teen moms grow and change throughout the years.

Here are five practical steps to running a Teen MOPS group:

1. Feed them and give them a break.

The first practical step to leading a Teen MOPS group is to meet each young mom's basic needs. It's really hard to sit through a meeting when your stomach is growling. It's also really hard to sit through a meeting if you're trying to care for your baby at the same time.

We provide a meal for our moms on most nights. We have groups or individuals sign up to bring meals, and about half of our meals are provided for us by people other than our leaders. Pizza and snacks work for the other nights!

We also provide free childcare for our moms. We know young moms are often tired and need a break; knowing loving volunteers are caring for their children allows them to relax and enjoy the meeting.

In addition, we have a baby store filled with donated items, and we provide diapers every week. Basically we want to help them provide for their baby's needs and give these moms a little peace and less to worry about in the process.

2. Wear a smile and make it fun.

Teen MOPS groups are made up of . . . teenagers. When they arrive, welcome them with a smile, and make the atmosphere lighthearted. Have a schedule, but don't watch the clock or get stressed about "everything getting done." (Remember: People are more important than activities.) Offer door prizes and do crafts every few months. The more relaxed you are, the more welcomed the young moms will feel.

3. Make it an atmosphere of learning and growing.

Teen MOPS groups are a safe place for teen moms to learn and grow. It's wonderful to bring in people to share inspiring stories or useful information, but let speakers know ahead of time that it's not an "us versus them" meeting. Instead, open up communication between the speaker and the moms early on. Before you turn the meeting over to the speaker, ask questions about his or her family. Help the teen moms see that this person is just like them. During question-and-answer time, encourage the leaders to jump in with questions of their own. Let the teen moms know we all have areas where we can grow and learn together!

4. Work through a book.

Work through a book such as *Teen Mom: Your Stronger Than You Think* and the free workbook! (zondervan.com/teen-mom)

Sometimes it's hard to broach certain topics with young moms, such as recommitting to purity, forgiving after being sexually abused, or bad boyfriends, but *Teen Mom* covers these topics. Reading the chapters and answering questions together helps you to broach subjects that might be too difficult to bring up. It also gives the teen moms a chance to open up and share their experiences as they talk through the answers to the questions.

5. Give them hope by sharing Jesus.

When I first started leading a Teen MOPS group, I was so nervous about saying the "J-word": Jesus. I didn't want to scare them away. I didn't want them to think I was some crazy Bible lady. But I've found they want to hear about God, prayer, and having Someone to hope in.

We start our meetings with a short devotional talk by one of our leaders. We have free Bibles and Christian books available. At the end of the meeting we gather in one big circle and hold hands, and then one of the leaders prays. Years from now a teen mom might not remember all the details about carseat safety or how to create a perfect job résumé, but I want her never to forget Jesus loves her and has good plans for her life. I want her to know God's Word applies to our everyday circumstances, and Jesus will always be there when we cry out to Him.

And I guarantee if you cover numbers one through four, they'll believe number five . . . because they've seen God's love lived out before them.

Your Turn:

1. What above steps will you implement in your next meeting?
2. Brainstorm a few new ideas to incorporate in your group.
3. Ask your group what they would like to do and learn!

Chapter 5

Finding Friendship at MOPS: You'll Be Blessed, Too

I attended my first MOPS group at my home church in Kalispell, Montana, in 1998. I was a mom of three young kids, and I loved hanging out with other women, getting to know them, and hearing wonderful speakers. OK, the crafts were good too.

My second year of MOPS I was asked to speak. I remember one meeting when I shared about once-a-month cooking. Yet as I shared about how my friend and I spent one day cooking 144 meals together, I noticed a young woman in the back of the room. She was a teen mom, and from the way she fidgeted I could tell she felt completely out of place. My topic was irrelevant, and my heart ached.

As a former teen mom, I remembered the feeling of not fitting in. I had a plan to make a beeline to the young mom as soon as the group was done, but she slipped out early and I never had the chance. I mentioned it to our coordinator, and that's when she told me about Teen MOPS. A support group for teen moms? I knew it was something I wanted to do. I was also bummed because I would be giving up "my MOPS friendships" to serve.

Our first Teen MOPS group started in 2001. There were thirteen leaders and two moms that first meeting. They next week we had four. The week after that eight young women. The group grew, and I saw God doing amazing things. Many young women grew close to God. They learned how to be better mothers, and friendships were made—friendships between the young moms, friendships between the leaders, and friendships mixed within both.

I have to admit things weren't always easy. The young moms had issues. There was conflict between them. We never seemed to have enough childcare workers, and there were times it seemed the young women weren't paying attention to a thing we told them. Some made one bad decision after another.

Yet as I poured out, God filled me up. I knew what I was doing was a way to glorify Him. Even if the young women didn't always respond like I'd hoped, I was loving those who so many others turned their backs on.

The years passed and friendships grew; in 2010 my family moved to Little Rock, Arkansas. I lived in a new place, but my heart was still drawn to the young moms. In fact—I discovered—Arkansas has the highest rate of teen pregnancy in the nation.

Our inner-city Teen MOPS group has been going for five years. We are serving young women who don't have dads in the picture, who often don't have the help of their baby daddies, and who live in poor areas high in crime. They are as different from me as can be, but they are my friends, too. We chat, we text, and I'm thankful to be a part of their lives.

Years ago I wanted to reach out to one young woman, and now every week I meet young moms who aren't sure they fit in. I thought I was giving up my friendships . . . but I've found new friends—both with the young women and the other leaders.

To be joined in a friendship is to have harmony, accord, understanding, and rapport. It's knowing each other and enjoying time together despite the differences. Or maybe it's not only putting up with the differences, but appreciating them.

Yes, serving in Teen MOPS is work, but it's also a joy. I'm blessed as I serve, and I call many of those blessings *friend*.

Your Turn:

1. Whom in your group do you want to make an extra effort to get to know?
2. Invite her to coffee, a play date, etc.
3. Let her know she matters and you are there for her!

Chapter 6
Why Does Mentoring Matter? A Lesson from Mary

Mary the mother of Jesus is one of the most well-known women of all time. She was also a teen mom facing an unplanned pregnancy.

1. Mary was signed up for a big task she wasn't prepared for.
2. Mary no doubt faced criticism from people around her.
3. Mary found someone to turn to, a friend who could help Mary succeed in her new role. It was Mary's older cousin Elizabeth.

Elizabeth played an important part in Mary's life. We know this because the book of Luke begins by telling us Elizabeth's story first. Elizabeth was the wife of a priest. She was very old and had no children, but God blessed her in her old age by allowing her to get pregnant. After Elizabeth's story comes Mary's story . . . another surprise pregnancy. Can you imagine what a shock that was to everyone who knew both women? (Yes! I'm sure you can!)

The cool thing is the angel Gabriel told Mary about Elizabeth's surprise pregnancy. It's as if he was saying, *"Look, there's someone in your same situation. Turn to her. She can help you."*

Mary did go to Elizabeth. In fact she lived with her older cousin for three months. Elizabeth was the first one who rejoiced over the child Mary held within her womb, and I imagine Elizabeth was there to encourage Mary as she coped with the idea of becoming a teen mom.

Like Mary, each of us should have people in our lives who we turn to for help, support, and encouragement. Being a mom isn't an easy thing, and facing an unplanned pregnancy is even tougher.

When I had my son Cory, I was seventeen years old, and there was a group of women from my grandma's church who supported me. They were the first ones who showed me the child growing inside me was a gift. They gave me a baby shower, and they fought over holding my son after he was born.

As my son grew, there were other women I looked to . . . and most of the time they didn't even know I was watching. One of them was Cheryl. Cheryl was patient with her children; she gave them big hugs. She laughed with them and played with them, and I modeled myself after her. **The thing about finding mentors is sometimes we can observe them without them even knowing. And if we're really lucky, they enjoy their role of giving us advice.**

Later when I had two kids, I met a friend named Cindy. She and I were the same age, and we became fast friends. Cindy was a support to me because we traded babysitting, talked about parenting problems, and encouraged each other. She was someone who was walking the same road as I, and her advice helped more times than I can count.

No matter who we are or where we live, each of us can look around and see the people we have in our lives. Some may cheer us on, some may guide our parenting, and others may just be there to walk alongside us. If the mother of Jesus needed someone to look to for support . . . shouldn't we? Everyone needs mentoring, someone to provide a little help and support.

Your Turn:

1. Who can you be a mentor to?
2. Who can mentor you?
3. What other mentoring relationships can you see in the Bible?

When it come to mentoring a teen mom, you never know what a difference you will make.

Chapter 7

Teaching Teen Moms About Sexuality Purity

There is one thing we know when a young woman joins our group. She has been sexually active. Young moms become sexually active for many reasons. Usually they are simply looking for love, yet sometimes it's more than that.

Most of the young woman I've worked with in Teen MOPS have a history of sexual abuse. Many of them don't remember ever being pure. Some have been raped or compromised in other ways. We often have to start with the basics when talking about sex, purity, and starting over to make better choices.

The basics:

1. **Be a role model.** The young people in our lives follow where we lead. Consider your life. Are you living with integrity? Are you only having sex within the bounds of marriage? The saying "Do what I say not what I do" never works.
2. **Talk about what love is.** Love is not sex. Going "all the way" with someone doesn't prove your love (no matter what they show on television). True love is shown through committing for a lifetime and valuing the other person. Remind teens they are responsible for setting sexual limits on a relationship. Remind young women, "Sex won't make him yours. A baby won't make him stay."
3. **Remind young moms it CAN happen to them again.** Having sex, even so-called "protected" sex, can lead to pregnancy. The only way to prevent pregnancy 100% is not to have sex.
4. **Let the young moms know know that most teens wished they had waited to have sex.** In addition to the physical, emotional, and economical challenges of having sex, there is emotional baggage. According to teenpregnancy.org, 60% of teens "wished they had waited longer" to have sex.
5. **Encourage a teen mom to plan her actions BEFORE the situation arises.** Talk about setting boundaries and not putting herself in situations that will cause her to compromise those decisions. Help her make good plans for her future and stick to goals. Remind her to think about what's best for her and her child.
6. **Talk about media's wrong messages.** The media (television, radio, movies, music videos, magazines, the internet) are chock full of material sending the wrong messages. Just because we see everyone in Hollywood having sex and having babies doesn't mean it's the right thing to do.
7. **Encourage secondary purity.** Teens can say "no" even if they've said "yes" before. Today you can make the right choice and choose abstinence.
8. **Realize mentors can only do so much.** As a mentor, you cannot be around 24/7. Yet, we can do our best to give young women the information they need. Don't wait.

Let young moms know you are available to talk these issues. Open up a two-way conversation, not a one-way lecture. Here are some questions to start:

What are your boundaries?
Do you think sex proves you love someone?
What do you think of the messages media gives?

Your Turn:

1. Which questions stick out to you? Write down your story.
2. Plan a time to talk with a young woman. Make sure she knows it's safe talking to you and you have her best interests at heart.
3. Pray together and let her know she can talk to you anytime she has questions.

Chapter 8

The ABCs of Supporting Young Moms

In September 2001, I was one of a dozen women waiting expectantly for the first teen mother to walk through the door. After working as a volunteer director of Hope Pregnancy Center for two years, I finally found a tangible way to meet the needs of teen mothers: through the launching of a Teen MOPS (Mothers of Preschoolers) weekly support group. The mentors grinned broadly when two teen mothers ar-rived for our first meeting. The next week we had four moms. The week after that, eight girls attended!

Now, two years later, twenty to twenty-five young moms attend every meeting, and we have more than five dozen names on our roster. These young moms come to make a connection with others in the same life situation. They also learn how to be better moms and women by listening to encouraging speakers and meeting with personal mentors. During our two years as a group, we've seen a number of teen mothers finish high school. Some have chosen secondary virginity. The greatest re-sult is that many have given their lives to Christ. Because of the large number of attendees, we're currently planning to launch a second Teen MOPS group! How did we do it?

Here are the ABCs of providing an encouraging and educational support group for young moms:

Assemble a caring team.
Many caring volunteers from our local PCC volunteered to help with the teen moms. Radio ads, community service announcements, and church bulletins helped spread the word and attracted volunteers. Former teen mothers, working moms, and even grandmothers from the community turned out. Those who believed in our mission and statement of faith soon found themselves holding babies and providing a listening ear to young moms in crisis.

Be diligent in training yourselves about the needs of young mothers.
Read books on teen parenting, talk to former teen mothers, and if possible visit other support groups to see what works. Get together with a teen mother, and you'll be amazed to hear about her unique challenges.

Consider a young mom's needs.
When planning our weekly meetings, we organize rides, meals, and childcare. We design fun games to introduce the young moms to each other, and we invite speakers such as alternative education teachers, job trainers, and child educators to provide informative talks. We also look for a neutral place to hold the meeting, such as a community center rather than a church.

Decide whom you want to serve.
We opened our meetings to young moms, ages thirteen through twenty-two. Yet we also allowed parents, grandparents, and boyfriends to attend if the young mom felt she needed extra support. We found these teen moms by taking flyers to alternative schools, doctor's offices, the public health department, and other low-income service providers.

Earn their trust.

Don't make promises you can't keep to the young moms. If you say you're going to call, then call. If you offer help in a certain area, provide it. Young moms have often been hurt by those claiming to care. Your follow-through will prove that you really do care.

Follow up.

Some moms come every week without fail. Other moms seem to drop off the map. Volunteer leaders are encouraged to call young moms to check up on them. We also send "missing you" notes in the mail. We've discovered that the times these young women don't want accountability are the times they need it the most!

Give special attention to their babies.

Young moms are more likely to receive condemning looks rather than enthusiasm over their children. Even though the circumstances under which these babies were conceived are less than ideal, the babies themselves are precious children, created in God's image! Rejoice over these little ones, and it will bring joy to their moms too.

Have open arms.

These young moms aren't perfect. They often say the wrong things or strike out at those who want to help. Yet, open arms demonstrate Christ's love.

Invite input.

Every few months we ask the teen moms what topics interest them. They've suggested such topics as "claiming parental rights" and "domestic violence." Getting input insures we're meeting real needs. It also lets us know what problems our clients are facing.

Judge not.

When our meetings started, we encountered women with pierced body parts, tattoos, and skimpy clothes. We didn't judge them or criticize them. We just kept caring and loving—never giving up. As these young hearts softened, their appearance often did too.

Keep the community involved in your group and your group involved in the community.

Our local PCC provides all the funds for our group. Likewise, we help the center with fundraising events. The young moms have served joyfully at banquets or have spoken in support of the center. This interaction helps the young moms witness the loving support from their community. It also helps the community see the difference we're making in young lives.

Listen to your heart.

If you notice a girl who is downcast or if you sense that something's wrong, take her aside and offer a listening ear. Many times our hearts pick up on pain, even when it is not voiced.

Make sure you seek help from experts.

When planning our group, we received help from MOPS International. MOPS provided manuals, materials, and experts to help us create the best group possible. Check them out at www.mops.org/teen

Never allow gossip.

Young women are good at "sharing," and sometimes the leaders have trouble with gossip too. Stomp out gossip quickly. If prayer is needed, share the requests with those you trust and take the requests before God together.

Open the floor for discussion.

In addition to good instruction, young moms need a safe place to share their concerns. After the speaker finishes, allow the moms to share their hearts' concerns in discussion groups. Remind them that everything shared in the group stays in the group.

Provide for their physical needs.

Teen moms need support and encouragement, but they also need practical items such as diapers, wipes, clothes, and baby furniture. We use the "Earn While You Learn" program to help these young moms earn items for their children. We also give extra "Mommy Money" for attending meetings and bringing a friend.

Question what part each leader should play.

Some leaders love getting into deep conversations with the young moms. Others enjoy cooking or working in childcare. Encourage each leader to follow her gifts. Each task is important.

Require responsibility.

Our doors are open to any young mom, but we ask her to take on responsibility for being part of the group. Young moms help set up and clean up for meetings. They also must be responsible for their words and actions. To make it a safe place, we require each young woman to behave respectfully and responsibly.

Set Boundaries.

There are some young moms who would never ask a favor. Others push the limits. Leaders are not babysitters or chauffeurs. Setting boundaries in the beginning helps keep leaders from getting overwhelmed. Rules also give leaders a way out when requests are made.

Trust they are listening.

Sometimes the young moms seem more interested in everything but the speaker, yet I've discovered that they often are listening even when it doesn't seem so. Months later I sometimes hear parts of previous discussions in the conversations among the young women. It warms my heart!

Use resources they can connect with.

When I started working with teen moms, I had a hard time finding resources specifically for them. That's why I joined up with MOPS International to write *Life Interrupted: The Scoop on Being a Young Mom* (Zondervan). This book focuses on the needs of our youngest mothers. There is also a free group leader's guide available from MOPS.

Visualize where you see these moms five years from now.

How can you help each one be a success? Share your dreams, listen to theirs, and prod them on.

Weigh your motives.

Sometimes it's easy to get discouraged when we don't see immediate changes. It's good to ask: "Am I focusing on where God is working or on what I want to see?" Often we'll never see the impact we make, but God is faithful!

Xpect challenges.

Any time you share the love of Jesus, you will come across opposition. Deal with the opposition through prayer. Pray for the babies, for the other leaders, and especially for the young moms.

Yield to 'good enough.'

As leaders we will never run a perfect meeting or say all the right things at the right time. Know that the love you show is good enough to make a difference. Also know that in your weakness God's strength will shine!

Zero in on the young mom's heart.

It can be discouraging when a young mom drops out of school or maybe even becomes pregnant again, but it helps to zero in on her heart. Every young mom can be changed through the love of leaders and the love of Christ. We may not be able to see the changes for years, but know that each effort to show God's love will make a difference!

Make sure you seek help from experts. When planning our group, we received help from MOPS International. MOPS provided manuals, materials, and experts to help us create the best group possible. Check them out at www.mops.org/teen.

Chapter 9
Easy Ways to Reach Out to a Single Mom

Teen MOPS is a wonderful ministry, but it's only one way to serve teen moms. I know what it's like to be a young, single mom and what made a huge difference caring people made in my life. Here are some ways you can reach out to single parents . . . and encourage your church to do the same:

Free childcare.
A moms' day out is greatly needed! You should know these moms, especially teen moms, may have a hard time leaving their children. Outline for them as clear as possible who will be watching their kids, what type of childcare experience they have, and what activities will be done. Many young moms have been hurt in the past in numerous ways, and they are very sensitive when it comes to their kids.

Guy events.
Many children of single parents don't have positive male role models in their lives. Think of activities for guys to do with kids: fishing, an obstacle course, Lego building, etc. All of these would be a huge blessing for the moms. They understand this need in their kids and feel bad because of it.

Car clinics.
Many single moms don't have someone to help with maintenance like checking the oil, checking the tires, checking the windshield wipers, etc. Cleaning out and detailing her car would be a huge blessing to a single mom too.

Expert advice.
Do you have experts who could help them with advice?

- Legal (custody stuff)
- Résumé building or job training
- Parenting tips or help
- Cooking simple meals
- Reading the Bible

Pass out a questionnaire ahead of time and find out young moms' needs

Necessity Kits.
Many moms struggle with money. Kits you can put together should include:

- First aid kits
- Cleaning or toiletry kits
- Spice cabinet basics
- Home "office" kit: calendar, stamps, pens, tape, stapler, etc.
- Kitchen towels and potholders

Christian books and resources.
Again these are "splurge" items they're not able to buy for themselves.

Craft time.
Single moms often don't have time to sit down and have fun. Create a craft event where they can sit, make something cool, and chat with others.

Gift cards
Give them a gift card for dinner out at someplace other than McDonalds.

Gas cards.
They often get stuck at home because they don't have enough money for gas.

Christian music.
They usually don't know it exists but find it uplifting.

Toys-R-Us or Walmart gift cards.
So they can buy something nice for their child's birthday or a holiday.

Home improvement projects.
Mowing the yard of a single mom or putting together a set of bunk beds is a huge help.

Offer a mini-vacation.
This takes more work, but moms often don't get a change to get away. Does someone you know work at a hotel chain where you can get a discount on a hotel room? Or does someone have a vacation home or time-share nearby?

Invite her to your house for dinner.
She'll be happy and shocked!

Free haircut, manicure, or massage.
. . . from a professional! Being pampered is something they usually don't have the time or money for.

Kids haircuts.
This is a huge help to her too!

Birthday cakes.
Do you have someone who can bake a birthday cake for her birthday or her child's?

Your Turn:

1. Who can you reach out to this week?
2. Pick one or two things you know that person needs?
3. Call that person up and tell them how you'd like to help. You won't regret it!

Chapter 10
Make an Impact Today: Follow Your Passion

Do you want to make an impact? God has put that passion in you for a reason.

James Hudson Taylor was a well-known missionary to China in the 19th century. What people may not realize is that his decision impacted his family to serve the Chinese people for nine generations! And it all started with one man's burden.

Hudson Taylor was weary and ill and had gone to visit friends in Brighton, England, where he hoped to find rest and spiritual enrichment. It was Sunday, June 25, 1865, and he had accompanied his friends to the morning worship service; but Taylor was "unable to bear the sight of rejoicing multitudes in the house of God."

He left the meeting and walked down to the seashore, his heart greatly burdened. How could so many believers be joyful and yet do so very little to share that joy with the lost, especially the lost in China? On that Sunday morning, Hudson Taylor resolved that, with the Lord's help, he would begin a mission to reach the lost of inland China. Two days later, he went to the London and County Bank and with a ten-pound note opened an account in the name of the China Inland Mission.

That piece of Christian history reminds me of what Jesus did, as recorded at the end of John 8. It was the last day of the weeklong Festival of Booths, and the people were celebrating in the temple. At the same time, their religious leaders were rejecting their own Messiah, who was standing among them; in fact, they were on the verge of stoning Him! Undisturbed, Jesus calmly departed from the temple area and obeyed Isaiah 42:7 by bringing light to a blind beggar: "To open eyes that are blind, to free captives from prison and to release from the dungeon those who sit in darkness."

Maybe like James Hudson Taylor you have a burden you can't shake.

8 Ways to Have an Impact for Generations

Pay attention to the burden God has put on your heart. Is there an issue that rubs you the wrong way? Is there a need you can't stop thinking about? Perhaps you can relate to the cause. I'm passionate about helping teen moms because I used to be one. My friend Kayleigh is dedicated to reaching out to women caught in human trafficking because she was victimized as a young girl.

Ask questions. If you could do one thing to help others, what would it be? Turn to God and ask Him to show you how you can help. I helped start a crisis pregnancy center in 1999. I'm good about sharing the passion and connecting with volunteers. Today I'm using those same skills in my work with our teen mom support group, but I wouldn't be doing what I'm doing if I hadn't asked, "God, what can I do?"

Take the first step. Every impacting ministry or outreach started with one first step. Maybe you need to seek out a professional organization for guidance. Maybe you need to talk to a pastor or friend about your passion and seek their advice. Maybe you need to read a book on the subject. The hardest step is usually the first one, but as you take next steps it becomes clear.

Be the expert. Passion only gets you so far. Knowledge points you to where you need to go. It also gets others on board. Even though I was a teen mom, I only knew things from my perspective. Once I started researching teen pregnancy, I became an "expert" on how ordinary people could help young women. As I became an expert, I had the confidence to help. I also had the confidence to share the need, my passion, and the solution with others.

Realize it all depends on God. God didn't give you this passion and then say, "There you go . . . have fun trying to make it work." God put the passion for a cause within you, and then He seeks to give you the wisdom and strength to make a difference. You don't have to do everything yourself; depend on Him!

See success through God's eyes. We want to make an impact, and often we think this means making a BIG impact. Jesus could have waved His hand and healed multitudes at a time. Instead, He reached out and touched individuals, focusing on that person in that moment.

Focus on the one person in front of you. Show him/her the light. There will always be more needs than what we can meet. We can't help everyone. There will be an end to our resources. But you can help one, or two, or twenty with God's help.

Realize your greatest work is passing on the flame. We can only run so far for so long. Think of making an impact as passing on the flame like those who help carry the torch for the Olympics. I helped start Hope Pregnancy Center, and I've started Teen MOPS support groups. Throughout the years hundreds of people have volunteered and continue to volunteer. It's amazing to know a ministry will continue, even if I move or if I'm out of the picture. It's not about what we can do; it's about what we can do together.

What about you? What is your passion? What type of impact do you want to make?

Lessons for Teen Moms to Remember

When it comes to Teen MOPS meetings we don't need to bring a speaker to every one. Sometimes the best lessons come from our own experiences.

Here are five lessons for teen moms to remember. Read these sections in your meeting, then open it up for discussion. Share your thoughts, and take time to listen to theirs.

Make Good Choices
by Tricia Goyer

You've made good choices already; trust you will make more.

Teens make good and bad decisions every day. Lots of them. Most aren't as visible as teen pregnancy. Perhaps you think it's unfair. Your choice is leading you to make choices you weren't prepared for.

You may not have been prepared to be a teen mom, but you can be a good one. By choosing to have your baby you're already taking responsibility. You're choosing life for your child—you're trying to do your best.

You may not have all the knowledge, resources, and wisdom, but look around for someone to help you find what you need. You've made good choices already, teen mom; trust you will make more.

I turned to God when I was a teen mom because a group of women poured love into me. I was unlovable. Those women kept loving, even when I turned my back on them, and eventually my heart softened—to them and to God.

You may not have been prepared to be a teen mom, and others are dealing with the same emotions. Do you know another young mom in the same situation? Reach out to her. Give some time. Offer a listening ear. Affirm her good decisions. Seek help together.

Today is the day you can make a good decision. Today is the day you can reach out to another mom. Today IS the day you are loving your child. Trust that as you do more of all three, it'll be easier to do them more.

Discussion Questions:

1. Do you have a hard time looking past your mistakes? List as many good choices you've made you can think of.
2. What is one positive step you can take this week?
3. How can your parents or mentors best support you in this?
4. Is there someone you know who is going through the same thing? Someone you can meet up with and share your story? Find ways to use your story to help others.

You Are More Than a Statistic
by Tricia Goyer

Forty-three years ago there was a single, young woman about to give birth. She was young and didn't know how she could afford a child without her parent's help. She hadn't talked to her former boyfriend in months. She had no idea how to reach him, how to tell him she was having his child.

This young woman attended church some, yet her dialogue with God was stilted. How could God let this happen to her? What would her life be like now?

A baby girl was born, and upon holding her child this young lady knew things would be OK. Perhaps this baby was a gift, not a burden as she supposed. So this woman raised her daughter the best she could, and while she wanted to give her child more than she had . . .

. . . history has a way of repeating itself.

When the daughter became a young woman she found herself in the same situation—living at home, pregnant, scared. The daughter knew she could raise this child. After all, her mom had done it. But what would her life be like? How could God let this happen to her?

If you haven't guessed already, I (Tricia Goyer) was the daughter.

Born to a single mom, I as a teenager became a single mom myself. At age seventeen, I was blessed with a son. My boyfriend was out of the picture, and I faced raising a child alone with little education, no money, and, maybe according to the world, little hope for my future.

Now if you take this story at face value, I am nothing more than a statistic. According to government research, most daughters of young mothers go on to be teen mothers themselves. They face lives of hardship, living on welfare for the most part—becoming a burden rather than an asset to society.

Yet I am not a statistic. And you know why I'm not a statistic? Because God doesn't do them.

Did you hear that? God doesn't do statistics. In fact, He likes to blow them out of the water.

You see, God has a history of seeing something no one else does. Like seeing a king in a shepherd boy named David, seeing an apostle in a young zealot named Paul, and seeing a mighty warrior in a frightened nobody named Gideon.

God has X-ray eyes that see right through any outward characteristics or any national statistics. His X-ray eyes scan down to the heart.

And what did God see? He must have seen something worthwhile. Because . . .

At age 43, I'm a multi-published author of magazine articles, Bible study notes, curriculum, and fifty books. My book for teenage mothers was nominated for a prestigious award. I'm a national speaker, traveling to share God's good news.

While in my twenties I helped launch a crisis pregnancy center, start numerous abstinence programs, and launch support groups for teen moms.

Now, if I were not a believer, all these would be things I could really tout. But honestly, I can say it doesn't have to do with me at all.
It's about:

- A BIG God with BIG dreams.
- A God who has made an agreement with me that is eternal, final, and sealed.
- A God who is constantly look after my safety and success.
- A God who is strong in my weakness.
- A God who sees the future, sees the past, and has a perfect plan for me.

Well, I guess the whole truth is I do have something to do with it. It's only a little something, but I guess it makes a pretty big difference.

See, God can be all those things in my life, only if I let Him.

There is one thing I must do . . . and that is be available. Of course, I didn't just wake up one day and say, "Here I am. God use me." I didn't just clear my schedule and wait for God to show up.

Rather, the steps toward my availability were a work-in-progress. They started on the day I was six-months pregnant and accepted Jesus Christ as my personal Savior. I like to look at that as Day One.
If you don't believe in a BIG God with BIG dreams there's no use being available. But when you trust that fact—trust God completely, trust His dreams—THEN you can also trust Him to lead you to the right path.

Seeing God at-work. Seeing what He did with our lives when we were available made me hungry for more. I wanted to experience God at-work like that again.

Henry and Mel Blackaby say, "Watching the activity of God from a distance can never compare with the thrill of being fully involved in the Spirit's active work."

You have to want God. Not want to work for Him. Or learn about Him. But want Him. You have to want to experience Him at work in your lives. You have to be hungry for what only He can give—a hope and a future.

Discussion Questions:

1. Yes, your life took a detour, but that doesn't mean your life is over. What are some of your dreams you hope to accomplish?
2. What is one practical step you can take to start achieving those goals?
3. Pray about it daily and trust God will see you through.

God Isn't Punishing You For Your Past
by Tricia Goyer

The other day I was mindlessly scrolling my Facebook feed when a headline caught my eye: "Toni Braxton Once Believed God Gave Her Son Autism Because Of Her Past Abortion." My heart clenched as I read that—not only because of Toni's pain and shame, but *because of my own.*

As a fifteen-year-old young woman I found myself pregnant. Overwhelmed with despair and seeking advice, I went to a Planned Parenthood clinic. The "counselor" looked across the table and focused on my eyes. "You're young. You have your whole life ahead of you. An abortion is the best choice."

"But . . . what about the baby?" I'd asked.

"It's not a baby," she told me. "Right now it's just a few cells. The doctor's just scraping them out."

I bought into her lie, and I scheduled an abortion, even though deep down I knew it was a baby. I knew if I didn't intervene I'd be holding a child in my arms in seven months. And that scared me too.

Later I was horrified to find out that not only did those "few cells" have a beating heart, but little arms and legs and lips and tiny ears. Knowing that, the shame pressed down even more, and I walked through life feeling numb, unable to face the truth of my decision.

Then I found myself pregnant again at age seventeen. This time I was determined to carry my child. (I found out later many young women who've had an abortion have another baby within a few years. It's an "atonement child" of sorts.)

It was during this second pregnancy I turned my life over to God. I prayed, "God, if you can do anything with my life, please do." God has done amazing things. He gave me a beautiful son and later brought me a wonderful Christian husband.

Everything was going well in my life, but I still was ashamed of my past. Few people knew about my abortion, and I was sure they'd hate me if they found out.

A few years after John and I were married, I found out I was pregnant. I was so excited to have a baby with my husband. Finally, I'm doing things right. Yet a couple of months later I woke up in a pool of blood, and I knew two things:

First, I'd lost my baby.

And second, God was punishing me for my abortion.

Looking back, my heart aches for the young me, a woman who still didn't understand God's complete forgiveness. I saw God as a stern judge who was weighing all my deeds and found me wanting.

For years I felt my abortion was too much for God to forgive. I had a hard time forgiving myself. It was only when I attended a Bible study and worked through the book *Forgiven and Set Free* that I realized Jesus' death covered all my sins. Who was I to say my sin was greater than His sacrifice?

The freedom I'm walking in today comes from understanding who God is. My sin was horrible, yes. I'll always regret not having that child, discovering who he or she is and spending this life together.

Yet, I'm thankful for the eternity to come. I'm thankful in God's eyes I stand clean before Him, as white as snow. God is not a God who punishes us for our sin. There are natural consequences for our sins—pain and shame and regret were some of the consequences I faced—yet God offers forgiveness and grace. These are not dependent on who we are but on who He is.

As Romans 8:1–2 says, "So now there is no condemnation for those who belong to Christ Jesus. And because you belong to him, the power of the life-giving Spirit has freed you from the power of sin that leads to death."

Maybe you're like me. Maybe you are carrying around the pain and shame from past sin. And maybe you're thinking God is punishing you for mistakes in your past. If so, then do two things.

1. **In your mind's eye, go back to that moment of your sin.** See your sin, and then look to your right hand. Picture Jesus standing there. There's isn't a look of anger in his gaze, but one of compassion. He is there waiting for you to turn to Him and find Him so you'll have real, abundant life. He's been there all along, and He's waiting for you to give Him your whole heart.
2. **Picture Jesus on the cross.** See Him there. Know His sacrifice is enough. Pray and thank Him for that.

My prayer for you today, friend, is you will find a freedom in Jesus Christ you've never known before. I pray you will begin to understand the breadth and length and height and depth of God's love . . . not only for mankind, but also for you. Trust Him in that. Discover that truth for yourself today.

Discussion Questions:

1. Do you ever feel God is punishing you for your past?
2. How do you picture Jesus?
3. What's the difference between "natural consequences" for sin and punishment?

Finding True Love
by Tricia Goyer

I grew up going to church for the most part.

It started when I was eight years old and my mother and grandmother gave their hearts to the Lord. They attended a church where people attended together, yet they also reached out to one another outside of the church building. I remember picnics and dinners out. I remember a new community of people who surrounded our family with love.

I remember my Sunday-school teacher who shared God's love through flannel-graph stories and films. Not the VCR tapes movies, but rather the old reel-to-reel films that showed the parables of Jesus and told what it meant to be faithful, honest, and true. I loved my Sunday School class, children's church, and the prizes I got for memorizing Scripture. I remember singing songs about God. I remember wonderful summer VBS camps and memorizing the books of the Bible to win a board game.

The problem was that while all those things made me think about God (and I loved Him in a way), I didn't understand what a personal relationship God meant. I didn't know how it applied to my everyday life.

Instead of continuing my relationship with God and continuing to spend time with others, I walked away from that in my teen years. I wanted to do things my own way. I was looking for love, and I thought I could find it in boys.

Instead I found myself pregnant and without a boyfriend when I was only seventeen. For many, many months I didn't want to think about what God thought about me. I tried to push all thoughts of Him out of my mind. I didn't want to think about all the memory verses I'd memorized as a child. Instead, I wallowed in everything I had lost: my youth, my teen years, my boyfriend who was with someone else. I felt more and more depressed as they days passed.

Then one day around noon I was watching soap operas, and I started to remember those good moments when a church family loved me. I didn't dwell on everything that had gone wrong.

This day, I thought about a time in my life when things used to be right, when I was happy. When I believed in God, when I had joy.

And that is the day I gave my heart to the Lord—my whole heart.

I wrapped my arms around my stomach, and I said, "God, I have messed up big time. If you can do anything with my life, please do." It was at that moment I felt HOPE spring into my heart. Hope in God. Hope in my future. Hope in eternity because I knew Christ had forgiven me for all my sins. And that was the beginning of my love relationship with God.

Once I realized the depth of my sin and understood God had washed me and made me are pure and white as snow, that's when I truly fell in love with him.

We can have knowledge of God and spend time in His house and with His people, but until we understand who we are without Him—understand the truth of our sin—that's when the true love relationship begins.

By accepting my sin and the pain it caused, I truly fell in love with Jesus for taking that sin away through His death on the cross.

So let me ask you . . .

When did you fall in love with God?

Discussion Questions:

1. What experience have you had with church?
2. Is it possible to go to church and not have a relationship with God?
3. What does having a relationship with God mean to you?

23 Ways to Be a Good Parent by Tricia Goyer

When I was twelve years old, I was frustrated with my mom about something.

"I'm going to write down how to be a perfect mom," I told her. "And I'm going to keep it so I won't treat my kids this way!"

"Go for it," she told me. "And I bet you'll change you mind about the things on your list once you have kids."

I started that list, but I never finished it. I wish I would have. I bet they were things like later bedtimes and watching all the popular movies. And my mom was right. That list would have changed, especially since I know now there is no such thing as a "perfect" mom.

I love this quote by Jill Churchill: "The most important thing she'd learned over the years was that there was no way to be a perfect mother and a million ways to be a good one."

I'm sure there are a million ways to be a good mom, but (with the additional help from my Facebook friends) I've come up with twenty-three!

23 Ways to Be a Good Parent

1. Be patient. —Verna
2. Look at your child's eyes when he talks to you.
3. Tell him, "God has BIG plans for your life. I can't wait to see them!"
4. Listen to your children. Believe in them. —Molly
5. Give your child a way to serve others . . . and praise her efforts.
6. Play his favorite board game even if it's your least favorite.
7. Be willing to admit you were wrong—apologize to your children. —Billy
8. Read to your child fifteen minutes a day.
9. When you are spending time with your children, be there 100%. No phones or distractions. Show them how it feels and teach them to give that gift to others. Time together, quality time, is so important in our busy, doing-so-much world. —Shanyn
10. Make family dinners around the table a priority.
11. Learn how to say no and stick to it. —Bonnie
12. Love his father/mother.
13. Become a detective and discover your child's unique gifts and talents, and then help him or her to develop them!
14. Focus on training more than discipline/punishment. Keep the training spirit. Don't assume you've told them once or a million times and now they will never fail. —Angie
15. Speak with kindness.

16. Breathe! —Elizabeth
17. Kids need your direction. Be the parent not the friend. They have friends. —Cherie
18. Take time to answer your child's questions.
19. Always, always, always love them always. —James
20. Love and accept your kids, no matter what . . . and make sure they know you do. And hug them. Boys especially need love, acceptance, and more physical touch than the occasional spanking. —Mark
21. Listen to your child, the way you wish your parents had listened to you. —Dena
22. Take your child to lunch and leave your smartphone in your pocket.
23. Spend more time playing with your kids and their Christmas presents than cleaning up the wrapping paper mess.

Discussion Questions:

1. Which piece of parenting advice sticks out to you?
2. What is one piece of parenting advice would you share with others?
3. Ask you child what would be on her list; it will bring up some great conversation!

Bonus Materials

Other Questions You May Have

What are some of your methods to enlist volunteers?

- Church bulletins
- Local Christian radio
- Facebook
- Word-of-mouth

What are the training procedures for new volunteers?

We have a yearly training in August. It's usually a Friday night and Saturday event. I go over training materials (provided by MOPS International), and I answer questions Some years we try to go to the MOPS convention too. We have an application for leaders, as well as perform a background check.

What do you do in order to publicize Teen MOPS?

I've sent press releases to the media. We send brochures to doctor's offices, WIC offices, and other public service organizations. We send information to schools and churches, but we get the most girls by word-of-mouth. They tell their friends and invite others.

What steps do you take in order to evaluate your ministry?

We keep track of the diapers and resources we pass out. We keep attendance. Also, we have a weekly leader's meeting where we verbally evaluate how it's going. But the greatest evaluation are the lives of the teen moms. We can SEE improvement, and many have given their lives to Christ. We see them making positive changes. And when they invite their friends that's a very good sign!

Interview with Tricia Goyer about Teen Mom

CBP: *Teen Mom* **is a book for teen moms, written by a former teen mom. You also interviewed young moms all over the country. Why was capturing the heart of young mothers important for you? Why did you want to write a book just for them?**

Tricia: As a former teen mom, I remember what it was like not to "fit in." At seventeen I still felt like a kid, but I had a child to raise. It seems that no matter where I went, I always felt like the odd man out. At Lamaze class everyone was with a spouse, and I was with my mom. Parenting books had ideas like, "Have your husband watch the baby while you take a long bath." That wasn't an option for me, and it's also not an option for the young moms I work now with. I wanted to write a book just for them. I wanted to give them a voice concerning their unique struggles, such as dealing with creepy boyfriends and trying to juggle work and school. I also wanted to show them they're important and they matter—even if they don't fit the mold of what society expects a "new mom" to be.

CBP: In this book you share your experience as a teen mother; what were some of the hardest things you faced as a young mother?

Tricia: I'd say the hardest thing to deal with were my feelings of shame. There are many sins out there, but pregnancy out of wedlock is one that sticks out in front of you, literally. You can't hide it. I remember the looks of other students in school. The looks of people in the grocery store. It made me want to escape into my bedroom and remain there for nine months!

Another difficult thing was the lack of confidence in society. I'd get rude comments from old ladies in the grocery store saying I wasn't doing something right. One lady made a rude comment about my son having a pacifier! Also, I felt I wasn't "heard" by professionals, such as my son's doctor. I took Cory in because he wasn't feeling well, and the doctor dismissed it as colic. They didn't trust my word that something wasn't right. It turned out my son had spinal meningitis, and it was only because of my insistence for them to take a closer look that he didn't die.

It's hard enough being a good mom, but I always felt on display—as though I had to prove myself.

CBP: When did you get involved in working with young moms in your community?

Tricia: In 1999, I help launch a crisis pregnancy center in my hometown of Kalispell, Montana. Right away we realized we needed to do more than just provide free pregnancy tests and counseling—choosing to carry one's child is just the beginning. I wanted to help moms be the best they could be. So four years ago I help launch a Teen MOPS program. Teen MOPS is part of the bigger organization MOPS (Mothers of Preschoolers) International. Our first meeting we started with two pregnant moms. The next week we had four.

After that there were eight. Then the program really exploded. It's great because most of those from the first meetings are still attending . . . and now they have toddlers. It's great to see the growing and learning taking place, not only with the kids, but also with the moms.

CBP: What changes have you seen in the young moms you work with?

Tricia: The first thing we often see is a softening of their attitudes. Some girls are scary when the first come in. They've been hurt, and they have a wall around their heart a mile high. They hardly talk and don't want to participate . . . yet they come, and this tells me we have something they're looking for.

Once the attitudes change, it seems the heart isn't far behind. Each meeting one of the leaders shares part of her personal testimony, but the main "evangelism" we do is just loving them as Jesus would and showing how our lifestyle is different because of Him. We've seen girls start attending church and Bible studies with the leaders. Some have given their hearts to Christ. It's amazing what short personal stories and a little love can do.

Of course, there is also the personal growth of the moms. We've seen them finish high school, get jobs, find their own apartments, and interact with their kids on a better level. It's like being eyewitness to the world opening up before them.

CBP: Your book is endorsed by MOPS (Mothers of Preschoolers) International. How else are you working with MOPS to reach young mothers?

Tricia: In addition to coordinating a Teen MOPS group in our town, I also help encourage the growth of other groups in my area and around the nation. I'm always available to talk to those who are interested in starting a new group. Also, I often speak at MOPS' International Convention. Then there is *Teen Mom*, of course. I want to do everything I can to get this book into the hands of girls who need it—whether they're part of a support group or not. It's not that it's "my book." What I really want is for young moms to find hope for their future.

CBP: *Teen Mom* is all about the unique needs of a young mother; can you share some of their greatest needs?

Tricia: Some of these needs include importance, growth, perspective, intimacy, and hope. Importance to know that no matter what society says, they can be great moms and a wonderful influence on their child. Growth is needed so a mom doesn't feel like she's "stuck" because of this child. She needs to know she can grow into the woman she's always longed to be. Perspective because too often a teen mom only sees obstacles ahead. She needs to see the future can be bright. True intimacy is a big need because most girls get pregnancy because they're seeking this closeness with another person. They need to know true intimacy is sharing your heart with another, including friends and family members. And finally, what young moms need most is hope—hope that is found in Jesus Christ. I could come up with 1,001 ways for these young women to become good moms, but the best thing I can do is point them to faith in Jesus.

CBP: There is a lot of talk about the problem of teenage motherhood in our country; just how many young mothers are there?

Tricia: According to teenpregnancy.org there are 800,000 new teen mothers every year. That's a lot of young women who need to know they matter, that they can be good moms!

CBP: If you could choose one truth the young moms come away with after reading this book, what would it be?

Tricia: It would be the truth that Jesus is the answer. He is the Prince Charming they've been longing for. He is the peace they've been struggling to find. He is the support and the strength for all the days they don't feel like they can do this "mommy" thing. He is what they've been wanting, what their heart is longing for most. That's what I want them to know more than anything.

Originally published on Christian Book Previews

A Ministry for Teen Moms: Lessons I've Learned

You're very passionate about helping teenagers, especially teen mothers. What life lessons have you learned as a young mother and how are you using that wisdom to help teens today?

I was a teen mom when I was seventeen years old, and it was during my senior year of high school. I was a cheerleader, honor roll student, and on the outside I looked like I had my act together. When I got pregnant I remember just being depressed. My boyfriend broke up with me during that time. I dropped out of regular school and started doing community classes at home. It was a really tough time for me. I didn't want to talk to anyone. I didn't want to see anyone. I would sleep in until noon and watch soap operas. It was a hard time but my mom and my grandma's Bible study group started reaching out to me. They invited me to Bible study and had a baby shower for me.

When I work with teens today (I have a weekly support group for teen moms), I just encourage them to reach out to people and to let people support them.

I just encourage them to think about their future and know they can achieve all [their] dreams—all the dreams they thought of when they were a little girl: what career they wanted to have, what families they wanted to have. Just because they're pregnant during their teen years doesn't mean they can't make changes. Any day is a great day to start over and to start stepping out. I really encourage them to write out what those dreams are and then just take the first step.

If they want to go to college, maybe they should have someone go with them to the financial aid office to see if it's even possible. Or they can look at a catalog of classes. They can go on and do great things.

That's a great message to share with them. You mentioned you had support from your family. Do you find most teen mothers don't have support at home?

Right away it's a shock, so their parenting might be giving them messages of "You've ruined your future. Nothing good is going to happen now. That guy is no good for you."

I tell the girls to give their parents time to get used to the idea. Some parents will come around, some parents won't. Just know there are people out there in the community who care and want to help.

It is difficult because you don't know where to start with teenage girls who are pregnant. They need help with their education. They need rides to their doctor's appointments and WIC appointments. They need help with school. So it's a big problem.

How has your faith in God helped you to mentor others?

I think it's the reason I'm able to do that. When I was a teenager I was heading in the wrong direction. I mean boys and parties and just trying to make myself happy with all these things. It was during my teen years when I gave my heart to the Lord and I told him, "Lord, I give you my life, I have messed it up big time and if you can do anything, please do something with my life."

He has done amazing things. Just bringing those women [from my grandma's Bible study] into my life—they were the reason I looked to God. I saw their love for me. I thought, "If these women could love me, then maybe God can too." Afterward he brought a wonderful husband into my life. We got married. So many times you want to kind of forget past mistakes and put those things behind us and just go on with who we are now. As I started growing in my relationship with God, I felt God calling me to help mentor teenage moms.

There's a story of a young woman who was going to have an abortion. She had scheduled an abortion at 3:00, and a friend of hers had texted her mom and told her she was going to have the abortion. Her mom got her and asked her if she would go to a clinic—and she did. They went in at 1:00, and she got the ultrasound and counseling; she missed her appointment for her abortion. She actually had her little boy!

Originally published at BeliefNet.com.

Room to Breathe:
Reflections from Teen Mom Kayleigh

Kayleigh is a special young woman in my life. I'd give her more of an introduction, but you'll see why she's so special to me from her own words. I will say that if God has put a young person on your heart, step out of your comfort zone and become a mentor. You'll never know the full impact until eternity.

As I sit here in my room and think back, it's overwhelming for me to see how much we have been through and how much others have stepped in and helped us. As a little girl of sexual, mental, physical, and emotional abuse, it was very hard for me to trust anyone. Those closest to me I usually pushed away. But this one amazing lady kept loving me, no matter what I did and how I acted. And frankly, it was a little weird! As a fifteen-year-old who just gave birth, I was hurt, lost, and broken… yet she still loved me for me. That "lady" is a well-known author named Tricia Goyer, and she knows all my dirt. I will never forget me seeing the reality of me; it sunk in while I read an article called "Awaiting The Transformation." I now call this lady my mom.

Nathan, who is now my husband, and I had ton of baggage from our parents. *So why on earth did God place us together?* Well, I'll tell you a little bit about how much God does and will change those who are willing!

In the book Breathe, Nicole Bromley talks about mentoring . . . and the more I read it, I can see how all things really do work out for the glory of God! Nate and I were fifteen-year-old parents and so hurt from our past. The thing we needed most were people whom we could look up to and, in Nicole Bromley's words, could "breathe new life into" us.

Tricia breathed hope into our lives for three years before we even thought of making any changes. I hate to think of what would have happened if she would have become frustrated and given up after a year or two.

"We have to know the person who we are dealing with and that takes time," says Nicole Bromley.

If you're trying to help someone, don't just go all in and start telling her what to do or how to "fix" things. Instead take time and get to know the person and her exact situation.

If Tricia would have just said, "Why are you living together? Don't smoke; it's bad for you. Can you be nice to the other moms?" I would have pushed her away. Instead, she spoke a little at a time and *loved* me for me first. Soon I had space to breathe!

"Being a person who is available, welcoming, nonjudgmental, and authentic stands out like a familiar face in a crowd of strangers," writes Nicole Bromley.

I don't know how many times I would call Tricia day or night with questions or problems that were tearing at my heart. And not once did she say, "Can I call you back?" Not only that, but Tricia's husband, John, had open arms for us as well. He is the male influence that has helped my husband be the man he is today. They never judged and always had time, and trust me—it took time for us to let them in!

"Once I knew that she wasn't going to give up on me, I knew I could trust her. She always tells me that she is never going to stop loving me, caring about me, or being there for me. For once in my life, after being so hurt and misled though love and trust in my childhood, I could actually allow myself to believe it," a young woman wrote in *Breathe* about her mentor. When I heard, "You can do it, Kayleigh," I believed it!

So even if you're sick of this person you're trying to mentor . . . *do not give up!*

"Not only did she believe in me, but she also helped me to begin to believe in myself. She never let me say 'I'm giving up,' even though that's what I felt like doing. She made me see that there's a light at the end of this and that my life will be richer because I allowed myself to face the truth," said Nicole Bromley.

All because these two loving people got down to our level and got down and dirty in our mess, we can now say, *Yes, we can do it!* We learned this through the marriage classes they made us take, the Sunday dinners at their house, the wedding they gave us. Papa John (my dad) even performed the wedding ceremony. I can say, Do not give up! God is good!

What a mess we came from, but because of mentors, we have not only found the *love* of God but we are able to see things in HIS perspective.

"I have a burning desire to return the favor by investing myself in the lives around me. I long to make the same level of difference in someone else's life and future. This explains why so many mentors do what they do. They long to give from what they have received," said Nicole Bromley.

So I encourage you to step out, make time for others, and get to know them before giving advice. Love on someone today because you just may be the person to bring a breath of fresh air into her heart. Offer a hurting person a place to breathe!

"Preach the gospel at all times. Use words if necessary." —Francis Assisi
Romans 8:28

The Message (MSG) Meanwhile, the moment we get tired in the waiting, God's Spirit is right alongside helping us along. If we don't know how or what to pray, it doesn't matter. He does our praying in and for us, making prayer out of our wordless sighs, our aching groans. He knows us far better than we know ourselves, knows our pregnant condition, and keeps us present before God. That's why we can be so sure that every detail in our lives of love for God is worked into something good.

My name is Kayleigh. I am from Coarm, Montana, "the gateway to Glacier National Park." I was sexually, physically, verbally, and emotionally abused and used, which lead to teen pregnancy at the age of fifteen and again at eighteen! My husband and I found Jesus and got married at eighteen! My baby daddy (now hubby) and I are currently going on year fifteen, and I love him more each year! We have been through more than words could ever say!

Awaiting the Transformation: Seeing God's Plans Unfold

Sometimes I wish God would let me see a preview of how the ways I give, serve, and love will one day pay off. Such a preview would have been helpful when I first met Kayleigh.

I was volunteering at our local pregnancy resource center when her mom brought her in. At 15, Kayleigh had recently birthed her first child. Bad first impression. It's easy to judge people based on their behavior. From the first moment we meet someone, we label his or her actions. Good or bad. Challenging or trouble-free. In Kayleigh's case, she demanded rides to the teen-mom support group I'd invited her to. She picked out the best for her baby without a please or thank you. She clashed with other teen moms, talked instead of listened, and continued a promiscuous relationship with her boyfriend. It wasn't long before she was pregnant again.

You can imagine my judgments about her. Thankfully, God saw Kayleigh's potential when I could not. In fact, as I turned to God about her thorny personality, He showed me what He saw: a young woman hurt by everyone she loved, but a bud He hoped to bloom into a rose. A hint of change.

God first gave me a glimpse of Kayleigh's changing heart one night when one of the other mentors asked Kayleigh why she and Nathan weren't married. Even though they were only eighteen, they'd been together three years and had two children.

"I've always dreamed of a Cinderella wedding," Kayleigh said. "Nathan works every evening after school and on the weekends, but there's never enough money."

"Is that all? We can help you with that," I blurted out before I had time to weigh my offer.

The very next week Kayleigh invited herself over to work on wedding plans. Together, we picked her colors, designed and printed invitations, and created rice bags with tulle. Later, I was with her when she tried on dresses. The other support-group mentors got involved as well. We bought and prepared food, made bouquets, fixed hair, painted nails, and set up chairs on the big day. One mentor photographed the wedding.

Since that time, Kayleigh has become one of my closest friends, and it's a joy to see she's become a compassionate person who prays that her family and friends will discover what she's found. God transforms one life at a time. How do I know? I've seen it through Kayleigh. I also know because I've experienced it in my own broken past.

Each of the descriptors I would have originally given Kayleigh could have been used on me. Like Kayleigh, I had my first baby in high school. Like Kayleigh's, my flaws were easier to see than my potential. And like Kayleigh, I found a group of women who reached out to me, thorns and all, and showed me what the love of Jesus is all about. Worthy of the wait.

When I first worked as a volunteer in a pregnancy resource center, my aim was to save babies.. These days, I've also become pro-life about the other people God puts in my path. Even though I couldn't have foreseen the blooming of Kayleigh, God has reminded me of the value of every person. Even if they don't turn around, the "difficult" people are worthy of our attention. The teen mom. The troublemaker at church. The rebellious teenager. The family member whom no one wants to deal with. God has a plan for every person we label "difficult."

We may be privileged to watch God's plan unfold or be present when a new believer enters God's family. Or we may just be the ones asked to love, care, give, and serve with no guarantee of transformation. God doesn't give us previews. I think it's because He not only wants us to love those who will transform but also those who might never change. He knows when we give, love, and serve, changes do happen—mainly within us.

Originally published by Focus on the Family

Teen MOPS Wins the "Family Faith Builders" Award

At Mosaic Church's Teen MOPS program, young mothers attend weekly meetings where they build a relationship with Jesus Christ, learn parenting skills and gain peer support. Attendees earn incentives for participating, and can shop for diapers, clothing and other necessities.

It's amazing what the promise of diapers can do. As any new parent knows, the puffy, plastic-wrapped bale that's hauled home during the week's grocery shopping is essential—not to mention expensive. For a teenage mother, it's one more detail to be worked into her new normal.

Tricia Goyer knows this scenario well, because she was a teen mom. Now, as she goes about her work as director of Teen MOPS (Mothers of Preschoolers) at Mosaic Church in Little Rock, she can still summon up what it felt like to be in that position. "There is no stereotype as to what a young mother is. When I was in high school, I was a cheerleader, I was on honor roll, I had a lot going for me and I found myself pregnant," she says. "I had women who reached out to me when I was a young mom and I know that it really turned me around and got me on the right track."

In addition to peer support and incentives, Teen MOPS helps its members develop a sense of self and a relationship with Jesus Christ. As an author of more than 30 books, many on faith and family, Goyer is adept at connecting the dots between the omnipotent redemption available through Christ's love. "It's great just to let them know how important they are," she says. "Sometimes, they've never had anybody tell them 'You're special, God created you for a purpose and he has a good plan for you, he has a good plan for your life.'"

"Teens make mistakes all the time," Goyer says. "Pregnancy is one of those areas where not only is the teen mom affected but her child is impacted, too. And if we reach out, if we can help the teenage mother, encourage her, point her to good resources. If we can teach her how to be a good mom and a good role model, then we're impacting two lives."

Along with the aforementioned diapers (of which Goyer hands out about 1,600 monthly), young mothers also get a hot meal, inspiration from a speaker, prayer and peer companionship at weekly meetings. The group is made up of roughly 50 mothers, some as young as 14, of whom a dozen or so attend on any given Thursday.

Occasionally a group member has a supportive family, but many of the young women have been left to fend for themselves. Kayleigh Stoltz could be their poster child. At 15, she intentionally got pregnant as a means of escaping her troubled and abusive household in Montana. "I knew they wouldn't want a pregnant teen around," she says. "I went to a school dance and I got together with the first guy I saw."

She heard about the local Teen MOPS while in the hospital after delivering her daughter—like a lot of new participants, she went for the freebies and walked away with a lot more: "It was really cool to come to a place where these nice ladies were there to show you the basic things, like how to pack a diaper bag," she says. "I felt taken care of for the first time in my life."

One of the women handing out love and concern was Goyer, who founded the program Stoltz had stumbled onto in Montana. It eventually proved to be a match made in heaven. The bond between the two women is so strong that when Goyer and her family moved to Little Rock a few years ago, Stoltz wasn't far behind with her daughter, now 13, and her husband in tow. (She's married to the same young man she picked at random all those years before.)

Stoltz now volunteers at the ministry along with others who provide child care or cook dinner for the young mothers. Teens earn incentives for attending meetings as well as other positive activities, such as enrolling in higher education or attending doctor appointments. But as Goyer is quick to note, the material perks are a small part of the picture. "You know, those are things to draw them in, because we really want to share just how to be a good mom and what a relationship with God is all about," Goyer says. "We know that when you have those internal changes, that is even more important than providing diapers."

Originally published by Little Rock Family.

More Than a Play Date
by Nancy Kimball

Support program a lifesaver for local teenage mothers The Daily Inter Lake Kayleigh Stoltz was just 15 when she gave birth to MaCayla. A little over two years later, Audrieonna was born. For better or worse, the young Columbia Falls mother already was acquainted with what it takes to raise a baby.

"My brother is only 5 years old," Stoltz said this week, comparing her 4-year-old daughter with MaCayla's now-5-year-old uncle, "so I knew what to do."

And the young Columbia Falls mother had the constant support of her daughters' father, Nathan Stoltz. The two, now both 20, were married in August 2005.

She also was one of the first participants in the Columbia Falls Teen Mothers of Pre-Schoolers group, which still meets at 6:30 p.m. Tuesdays in Fellowship Alliance Church. They are, however, looking to the community for a new meeting place they can call their own.

Teen MOPS is where Stoltz hooked up with her one-on-one mentor, Tricia Goyer. Goyer founded Hope Pregnancy Center in Kalispell and started the support group for pregnant teens in Columbia Falls four years ago. Goyer had a heart for the girls then, and still pours herself into the local Teen MOPS - and into Stoltz.

"I spend a lot of time with the Hope House," Stoltz said. "My mom used to be a support, but I found out it wasn't the kind of support I need. And my dad's a child molester."

Her family life could have sucked her into a dark cycle. But with Teen MOPS, she rose above it.

Stoltz is one of the lucky ones.

Kimberly Heindel has had a tough time with life.

Heindel, now 20, has two sons - Tanner is 2 and Dustin is 8 months. She was married once, for a matter of months; her former husband fathered neither of her children. She had a couple of dead-end boyfriend relationships.

Last month, she was to marry another "kid," she said, but he got violent - enough to cause the tough young girl to break down in front of her Teen MOPS group.

"It broke the camel's back when he went after my oldest kid," Heindel said. "I didn't know it then, but he had all the classic signals of an abuser."

Now, she is with another boyfriend.

As a single, pregnant teen, she had no clue how to care for a baby when Tanner came along. Through books, videos, meetings and one-on-one help from Teen MOPS, she learned.

And she responded to the Christian faith foundation of Hope House and Teen MOPS.

"I was not sacrilegious, but I used to be the most anti-God," Heindel said. Then a car wreck started her on another long tumble. "God took away the car, the money … But now the more I pray, the more he comes through."

Today, her stepfather continues to offer steadfast support. So does Marie Johnston, her mentor with Teen MOPS.

"Our goal at Teen MOPS is to be there not just during pregnancy but afterwards," Johnston said. "That's the beginning of a new life, even if you adopt out. I was a teen mom, and I needed support after I adopted out."

But it's not just adults they need in this transitional time of life.

"We're helping them connect with other teen moms," said Columbia Falls mentor Kristi Siler.

Heindel said her circle of friends changed after her stepfather dropped her off at that first Teen MOPS meeting. Now she shares joys and struggles common to other teen moms.

Many of the earliest members of Columbia Falls Teen MOPS are moving on in life as they grow older. Their lives are improving, but the teen pregnancy problem is not going away.

In 2004, said Claire Beaver of Hope Pregnancy Center, 10 percent of all live births in Montana were to girls 19 and younger. In Flathead County, it was nine percent. In 2005, Beaver said Hope House had 1,403 "client contacts," instances in which they administered pregnancy tests, worked with teens in the Earn While You Learn program, mentored through Teen MOPS or other services.

It's the younger girls in the Columbia Falls area, probably pregnant and scared, whom Siler and Johnston are trying to reach.

"But those are the ones who won't go to a church," Siler said.

That's why the nonprofit Columbia Falls Teen MOPS is looking for a new home.

"We want to have someone give us a house," Johnston said. To offer pregnancy testing, it would need to be on property zoned commercial. "But we can start with a home just to have teen meetings, to hang out and have it be our place."

A couple of options already are available, but they need substantial renovation or removal to a new location - both costing money the group does not have.

"We want to get the community behind us because these are the community's kids," Johnston said.

Mentors also are needed, as are baby sitters during Teen MOPS meetings.

"The difference from having Teen MOPS in your community," Siler said, "is you have moms striving to do their best."

Made in the USA
Columbia, SC
26 August 2017